Like the Heart, the World

Sage Cohen

For Debbie, Queen of Wands

"Wisdom tells me I am nothing.
Love tells me I am everything.
And between the two my life flows."

– Nisargadatta

LIKE THE HEART, THE WORLD

ISBN 978-0-6151-5307-0

Book design, illustrations and typesetting by Grégoire Vion
www.grgwr.com

Acknowledgments

Thank you to the editors of the publications in which these poems first appeared:

Comet: . . . . "Where Besson Street and Chevron don't meet"

La Petite Zine: . . . . "Night of the Open Mic,"
"For You, Lost in the Night"

MARGIE: . . . . "God Says to My father"

New York City Streets in Poetry: . . "Without"

Open Windows 2006: . . . . "Algorithm"

Oregon Literary Review: . . . . . . "Queen of Wands," "Bukowski Hated Orange,"
"Sovereignty," "Sweetened Water Farm, 1989"

Poetry Flash: . . . . "Having Decided"

San Francisco Reader: . . . . "Like the Heart, the World," "Losing It,"
"Alchemy," "Nature and Psychology"

VoiceCatcher: . . . . "Apology," "Quantum," "I Make You a River"

Washington Square: . . . . "Exfoliation"

Contents

PORTLAND

New York

Thirst

We understand least
what we hold closest.

Cup contains, water resists.
Thirst: a lineage of cups

with no trust in the future.
What wakes you up in the night

mouth empty, sheets blank
might be the faucet's dumb neck

arched with a brassy assurance
that you have not yet learned to tap.

Exfoliation

A chorus of fat nervous birds
jitters on the rim of my table.
I offer them nothing.
Flimsy chairs scrape pavement.
A wind could take them. Underneath
bricks and bricks and bricks.
Along the endowed buildings
a neat stretch of fat flowers
combed into rows of receding color,
groomed pinker and pinker each spring.
But now it is fall and the statues are serious.
A copper horse, back arched, bites her tail.
She is green in her deep places.
I ask everyone who passes
if they know what exfoliation means.
Black and rivered says the first guy.
A skin condition says the next.
And finally *I'm just here for coffee.*
Cigarettes punctuate everything.
I light one and leave. Walk until I see
Washington Square Park's arch
standing two-pronged over the park.
A woman passes. She smells fake
like roses. Overalls mute the mercy
of her breasts.

Having Decided

daylight: wig over night's bald drone
nor does flesh offer a fresh opinion

once I cut a ravine, prayed
you'd wash through

instead my eyes learned to find you
in the white spaces

Pretty Lady Can I Get a Smile

I was busy setting myself on fire
when the truck came.

Pretty lady?
Pretty lady?

A small boy in a blue hood misses
a ball that is thrown to him.
A woman sitting on the fountain
looks like she's been stunned
into her business suit, a briefcase
thrust into her hand at the last moment,
as if on cue for something.

I got stuck in the middle
with the birds and the pacing men.
Pretty lady can I get a smile?

Maybe I should let the woman
in the Superman shirt with no
hair take me home while she
searches for the right adjective
to repair her marriage

I hid everything you could find
fault with in the back.
I like to walk on wounds
and wave to strangers
and count birds.

Your geography is impressive.
Do you know where your heart is?

I get this idea that nighttime
will protect me and curl
my hands into little hearts
against my face.

Oratorio

I have two souls.
One my mother gave me.
One the sound
of stones falling.

Messiaen singing through things.

The composer's arm
is the length of ribbon.
He devotes his body as I
devote my distance
to the sound
of stones falling.
The listener completes
the circle.

I am   at all edges
of sound   helping it breathe.

I am a woman peeling paint.

It was written for piano but I'm singing it.
Any bell opens the gate.
In the pause before opening,
a hundred years could pass.
A song could begin in the air.
Pigeons fumbling on ledges
like raisins in bread.
Dark sweet spots of pity.

I breathe in concentric
circles, the brief impression
a stone makes.
The widening circles
could be violin or Jesus
repeated so many times
that he becomes someone else.

Statistic

my blood unfurls its banner into the tub.
i will never come clean.

i write on white paper.
hand moving across the page.

cars blaze paved lines
through the exhausted air.

wanting and not wanting
are enemies of fate.

my heart the bullet
chamber. mind made small

by expertise, i cultivate
the absolute to extinction.

God Says to My Father

I don't judge you, so why
do you judge yourself?
My father sits smoking
in his black sports car.
Sits shrugging butterflies
off his suntanned arm.
Calling them moths.

Each Time the Sky Begins

I say *morning*
but it is death
making room for the body
the scraps of space
I do not fill return
to the sky like rain
to begin again

in this shallow blue and ash
a man with crutches drags
his withered legs
says to my passing back
life pulls, life pulls
the church hoists
its cross into the sky
along the curb dogs
hunch in intervals

I came to you vague
as to how
now I am the mouth
this city crawls through
you are the square the camera
took from the sky
stars develop in your hair

I will eat pigeon
and newspaper all
that flies I will give you
my legs and we
will walk like shadows
borrowed from light

Walking

I just want silence and a reason to laugh.
The trees have blown their kisses into the wind.
Everything is loose this spring.
Eyes rolling around in men's heads
when girls or the idea of girls
drop a shadow or a cigarette.

The spaces between things are white.
Perhaps they flower.
Perhaps they are pigeons
with greasy rainbow backs.
Tulips muck about in the loose sod.
The woman leaning on a cane stops,
unbuttons her sweater, drops
a crust for the birds.

I've got my camera.
Everything is more romantic on film.
There is no nausea
in the pregnant photos of me.
Just my new breasts
and his eyes on them.

Tulips open their throats
in fenced gardens.
What endures is not sexual.
The sexual is the flower.
Friendship is green
fast into the ground.
The ground comes up
through my feet.

Every good girl is dying to be trashy.
Wear black velvet dresses.
Nothing changes and the taxis come.

What is to become of a woman like me?
The sign blinks DON'T WALK.
Bags of garbage slump on a curb.
On the corner Jones Diner.
My brother is jonesing in Oregon.
I call him all the time and he doesn't answer.

The city is strange without the sun.
Rats bingeing on poison and oil.
Hunched backs
the small shrugs of this city.

Railings twirl in curlicues
along their stoop.
Umbrellas float like moony eyelids
through the wet streets and sidewalks.
A taxi takes the corner.
A shovel stands in a pile of sand, handle in the air.
Men muscling around in shiny hats.

Dogs and dirty windows.
Used up containers and men
scattered along the curb.
Hair everywhere.
A resounding *Yes! Yes!*
A man pointing to his ears, shaking his head no.

Without

The sky has swallowed the moon again.
Joe is doubled on the stoop
of Cucina Regionale.
I want to give him something
that he can keep. But nothing keeps.
Brothers die in fires or lose their skin
and the world is only slightly impaired.
Joe will be gone one morning
and the garbage trucks will come and when
the sidewalk warms we will sit
outside on folding chairs,
white napkins in our laps
and eat.

Uptown on the 1

I sit in a shiny orange seat clutching
Tess Gallagher's *Portable Kisses*.
I had hoped to find some kind of explanation
for what happens in love.
The train lurches forward toward
its predetermined destination.
On my hand, a tattoo that says
Jayne and Craig forever. It will fade,
as all promises do, with a few washings.
The man standing over me, holding his umbrella,
stares down into the darkness where my hair parts.
His ring and briefcase suggest that he is between
wife and work. I write this down, a faith
of naming. I am headed to 107th Street
where Shari lives, where her twins live
inside Shari, unfurling like fern tips
into the light. I wonder if they reach
for each other from across
their dim and distant sacs,
if they are warming up to the idea
of being born. No one sits down
to my left. There is too much of me there.
He is a pastor, not a priest, says the girl
to the man. They are leaning together.
I would like to belong somewhere.
Instead, I am traveling
between two apartments
that are not my home.

San Francisco

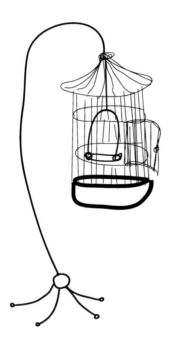

Like the Heart, the World

Like the heart, the world
expands and contracts.
We stand at the edge where
continent and ocean
overlap.

It is hard to know how to let go.
Cloud carries pink like paint
carries pigment. Each word, too,
enmeshed in the web of idea.

I walk with Amy along the beach.
The night blows its pinks in from the north.
As the sun sinks behind the furthest line
of ocean, the pinks settle
into the deepening distance
like a shucked skirt
slipped to the floor.
We walk into the wind.

Amy wears her mother's sweater.
It is not warm. It has a tissue in the pocket,
where one might presume
her mother expected to retrieve it.

We change direction and now
the wind penetrates our backs
like an old mistake that still aches.

The pinks are contagious. I want to surrender
myself here, let the flat mirror of beach break me.
Amy says it's the negative ions that feed us
what we need, make us exalted. But I think
it's the way absence echoes back at us
from the endless possibility of ocean.

Amy lifts her arms up over her head into the night.
Not prayer. Not flight. An opening.

She calls to her mother.

In this sky that includes beach and city,
past and present, dead and living,
pink is the language through which
Amy's mother answers.
Not because she has been called.
But because mothers will travel any distance
to see their daughters happy.

We stand with our backs to the city,
cloaked in the ocean's turbulent quiet.
There is a stillness. A kind of reverence among the pinks
as they settle in among the night's deeper darknesses.

We leave the beach and walk
into the night
as the final scarves of light
flare up and burn out.

Night of the Open Mic

In this corner store of war
men too many for membranes
music makes you manic.
You'd play pool. Drink or smoke
or some ruinous thing but you are
seven pages deep, all angles.
Were not honest about what you wanted.
A full suitcase to some new place.
What do we say to our smaller sanctions?
How does Brian stay alive?
What happens here happens everywhere. You sit
rimmed in tin, spinning until the straw
hat weakens without its weave.
Everything needs a pattern to keep the idea intact.
You need a room with music and the dancing
brimhatted lady. *I'm so wet* she says. Yes, she is wet
drenched in the night's darkness
and you are curling up in circles.
You need a band to back you up.
Lean into it and let it leave you.
Faces shushed to booze.
Just look at us. So much crap to wade through
to get to the little loose curls.
The woman laughs and calls you pretty.
The authentic is not easily achieved. The list is long.
Kyra opens the case and proves her point. You do what you say.
You're here to stay but don't like the music
but don't like the music, but don't like the sick skinny girls
who see signs when you see patterns.

Bukowski Hated Orange

but O'Hara devoted a poem to it
and SARDINES,
which art could not sustain.
Even LOVE loses its letters
in the slow descent
from art to conversation.
Maybe there's a way
to piece it all back together.
But where does what the man
was trying to say go
when meaning collapses
under the weight of expectation?
I wonder whether O'Hara had it right,
or Bukowski. One hoarded his letters.
The other crossed them out
until there was nothing left.

The Grief of the Violin

I lost you to your life
as a violin loses its music.

You moved through me
in the key of E.

The grief of the violin must be great.
Centuries of symphony

that can't be saved, played only
to disperse into individual notes.

Today you are a C. Bright and clean,
the knife with which I cut

my apple, the child on the swing.
I play you high and low,

but the note does not sustain.
Once, your hands were rosin

over me, smoothing the hinge
where our bodies met

as each note leapt
from the grooved

grace of me to take
its place in you.

Now the days are heavy
as quarter notes.

The songs grow thin
in the well of my throat.

Retrospective

It is too soon for clarity,
too late for truth.

You want to remember him
as someone you loved.

You move your body
to keep it alive while the man

ahead of you gets his brownie heated.
To go. To stay. The deception lives

in increments between
choice and action. You are not

who you were then. You are
not who you say you are.

You can't breathe so you breathe.
You need music and antibiotics

and whatever will make the facts more round.
The doctor says yes, you must try,

but he is only practiced
in the patterns of people.

The world has its own memory
whose entrances are curtained,

whose departures, like opera,
are holy and misunderstood.

For You, Lost in the Night

The imprint is what remains.
False, as it must be.
The reverse of shape.
The absence.

It is not the building. Not the love.
But what they represent.
The people they shelter.

I don't know where to call home or who lives there.

Is return ever possible?
Each time the door closes,
the house heals over and starts again.
Crossing its threshold, we become someone else.

The father goes to work and does not come home.
It is the expectation of continuity that destroys us.

Surely, this is a sickness.
Waiting at the site of the blast
for the illusion to repair itself back into form.

I say I am doing the best I can, but I am not.
I could do nothing. That would be better.
If I could be still, maybe something larger
than what I am trying to create
would emerge. The way a landscape rises up
around the curve in the road.
The way the family sits at the table,
without the father, and eats.

My Only Regret

said Eve, composed
of the bones of the man
she was born to receive,
is that before me came
the feast of garden where
understanding cost us taste,
where shape wept
for the memory of a man
who was once complete
as I wore the bones
that bore me without
making them my own.

The Irony of the Small Horn

Paul says the Great American Music Hall
should be called The Great European Music Hall.

Its gold flourishes and imperial balcony feel more
like something you'd yearn for from across an ocean.

Nothing is named right in this world.
I don't know what to call Paul's body against mine.

Dancing, maybe, but that's not enough.
It's more like a question before it is born

gathering force among the margins
of what is already known or believed.

Paul has his hand on my stomach where my shirt rides up
and I press into the beat coming through his chest.

My hips rotate with the room. Singular surrenders to plural.
Sweat and smoke and beer and bodies pulse in the darkness.

The music is a fire. Dancing is the flame.
We all depend on each other to burn.

Paul points out the enormous man playing the tiny trumpet.
All the big guys have small horns, we agree.

This poem was supposed to be about that. About the trumpet,
because that was how Paul and I planned it.

But nothing ever turns out the way you think it will.
The music ends, and then it's time to go home.

Nature and Psychology

The years line up like arrows,
pointing us toward somewhere else.
The days shine like paintings.
Perspective gives us near and far.
The poem began in a café
on Cole Street where you played
your guitar and I wrote
everything down because I believed
that truth could be conquered
with words. I had nothing to offer
but my future. You despised death
and exalted it, having lost more
than you were willing to give.
Ocean and coast cannot resolve
their attraction. It is this contradiction
that holds the world together.
The sky is a eulogy.
It holds everything. It holds nothing.
The tides recoil. Then they reach.
We're washed up on the shore.

Losing It

The dream said I couldn't have the baby or the worm.
So I swam against the current in my loose skirt.
Expectation unraveled to ocean.
Destination was many generations deep.
It was a surprise, my body's devotion.
Making its way forward
as if my survival mattered more
than what I could no longer carry.

Queen of Wands

Calling our beasts by their proper names
means letting go of hope
and its long-distance ecstasies.

Each rightful companion
has her own ending place.
Grief the graveyard of names.

In the open space, exchange.
I lost panther to gain leopard.
My hair let go of its color

and as I let go of my pain
even my leopard started thinking
she was someone else.

But I needed her more as witness
than as companion.
Her spots the doors now

closed to me, paths complete.
Though she yearns, my leopard
is too previous to become lion.

She waits for me on the shore,
sends her selves in circles out
along the smooth surface of my life.

Each day I drag her darkness forward.

Where Besson Street and Chevron Don't Meet

I am an unmarried woman.
My eyes fit together like a door closing
on an old life. See how the river runs
under me, the dog sleeps to my left?

I can't tell you how to get here
because I don't know myself
or which way you're coming.
I drive the neatly drawn line of Route 97.
Division Street divides us.

The difference between losing
one's maidenhood and losing
one's mind: ceremony.

The river comes in stages,
like death. Each day the sky wavers,
streaked along the bottom of things.
I curl to fit you but you are too long.
I let you sleep alone
with your face toward the river.

The trees wear a heavy fur of snow.
I wish I knew how to receive what is provided.
There are only alternatives, back roads
that refuse the heavy grip of tires, and kisses
that heap themselves like snow.
By morning, we are exhausted with the weight.

Sovereignty

riddled into remission
the hag yearns
for a chivalrous search

trained for persistence
Sir Gawaine unquestions
curse from fate

his answer her savior
the princess unfurls
to face the word that forgave her

Sweetened Water Farm, 1989

Some landscapes make you want to leave your life behind.

When night strikes its blues through you
and drifts a mood of moon over the water,
you think this silent boat
welling up with darkness could overflow
with the ache of the tree's stifled profiles.

Tonight the light thins
to a single line dividing
lake from sky.

Sail mute as a sleeping wing,
folded along the mast's proud spine.
The boat's heavy muscles relaxed.
You move through the layered blue
with your pale approach,
sink into the deep cavity of open boat,
push off beyond the buoys, docks
and all that might hold you.

The darkness makes all things equal:
wet plank, lusty pine, spindly sea bird
fluffed up and tucked along the night rim.

You are who you were and who you are becoming.

You know that memory, like any boat,
is filled with what we choose to carry.
That water will accept everything
thrown overboard.
First heft it up proudly,
a child on her father's shoulders
and then swallow it whole
like a mother's embrace.

Alchemy

Consequence and its heavy metals strive toward transformation
while imprecisely, a silent pine resonates with lake.

Among the assurances of proximity and place, she floats out,
weightless, over the lake's flat gaze. Heavy arms repeated and relieved.

Birds shape themselves to wind. The trees shift,
shimmering as snow sifts its silences.

Shadows send their slender semiselves out like wishes
that have not yet learned to lift. I sit doubled beside the pine.

A woman pleads with me from within the lake: *Leave* –
Listening to her is like eating a peach right down to the pit.

Everything green folds to gold and starts again.
Leaden is the death that does not find its way forward.

Harmony must first have been an opposition that stumbled
into agreement slightly above the departure.

Portland

Algorithm

Gravity borrows her name
from the bird who stopped trying.
He said the poem was a hinge,
that a bird fell into her womb
from the well. There is no law
that can convince me
otherwise. Call in
the scientists if you must
and name their theories
after themselves.
Our entire lives, after all,
comprise the world looking
back at us from beyond
our reach and saying this
is who you are.
Names the place markers
of what was last believed possible.
The dead tree leaps
across the water,
free of root.
I'm building up a tolerance
for the absence of proof.
Maybe there is some
straight line somewhere
confining us to the literal, but I
saw the bird's fear as something
useful, her blindness a kind
of guidance.

Quantum

Nothing is less real than realism...Details are confusing.
It is only by selection, by elimination, by emphasis, that we
get at the real meaning of things.

– Georgia O'Keeffe

From all possibilities: this
coat keeping warm from throat
to moment. Strung like street
from yellow line to yellow line.
The red-hatted lady sloshes by.
Not quite cohesive enough for story,
the notes hover like photographs.
Each one shouldering the weight
of articulation. My car shudders
with not enough. My eye sockets
dark as a harbor relearning
the art of return after war
stripped the world of metal and fear.
I should have given you a reason
to stay. I didn't see how
the trees could divide. I could give
you green. I could feed you fiction
The waitress asks me *Just one?*
as if I were not enough. And yet
the room can barely contain me.
There is no justice. And no waitress
to serve its unanswerable demands.

The Man

who was once
your doctor who
was once your
teacher but is now
just the person
you cannot accept
wrote down for you
his diagnosis. You shine
his words up
like little antique
albatrosses. Lift their
impossible wings, ornate
balconies of drift and rise.
You sprinkle them
like Italian herbed sea salt
over sweating cubes
of perfectly sized butter
to spread on the rolls made
by the man whose arms
are the perfect machinery,
whose mouth is Olympic size,
whose semolina beat France
with its unprecedented
sesame seeds
and flawless exterior.

Apology

the dogs have followed me
downstairs like heartbreak.
sadness is our habit.
i cannot find kindness
on the shelves.
i have no recipe.
only eggs and butter and faith.
there is no saving
grace, no blame,
no place of rest.
until i trust the sun
to its own descent,
forgiveness breaks me
down to dust the waves
carry me out over
the years i listened
to you leaving me,
the sound of it trapped
in my ocean ear
as the conch curls
her tidal heart
against the thin
shimmering of moon's
cinematic grief.

Sadness is Boring

says the champagne-dancing lady
in her evening gown fountain
statuesque among the gaze
of men and movies. Train tracks
heavy with hope, her smile
the fixed glint of sun
on metal, her mind smooth
as a well-traveled path and though
the trains have not yet learned
to heave their grief uphill,
the crossing awaits, shaded
in the patience of trees.

Bai Hua

There is a child in China.
I do not speak her language,
she does not speak mine.
What I hold are clippings
of her life in translation.
The day she admitted she had
something to say, someone wrote it down.
Rice could make the classroom beautiful.
She painted what the marker
could not sustain. Making beauty last:
Bai Hua's feet turn in as if she is traveling
into herself. In the off-kilter distance
faded in afternoon light she stands
slightly bent, one arm raised as if
she'd just thrown something
at the camera, or changed
her mind and wanted to erase
what was already said.
I know the metal taste of alone.
I would like to send Bai Hua my own
progress report for Spring 2004.
Sage has learned to ask for the colored rice,
it would say, *but realized she no longer*
needed it. She has stopped trying so hard
to camouflage her fear.

Bridal

The pond drifts its corsages
along the withered wrists
of trees fallen too soon.
The broken vow folds
its paper wings.
No boat, no confetti, today
the leaving falls away
to a float of daisies.
Each opens her hungry yellow
throat to the rain's staccato,
trodden banks, the simple
untamed thrill of hope.

I Make You a River

Philip Levine claims that there was at least one day when Lorca
and Crane were in the same place at the same time. His poem is the
imagined moment of flint on flint, as the poets' minds converged
in a small brush fire of tongue and ash before each fell forward
into his own, inevitable future.

Stranded in my own moment in time, the electric pulse of poetry
charging my clinging sweater, back lined up with the hard bench
of listening, I enter the eternity of Spring, where Lorca stands
stooped, his pockets weighted with unspent poems.

Each hard knuckle of bud containing a great courage of reckless
beauty unfurls itself into words under the spell of my recording pen.

Levine says: *horse cock and mattress stuffing*, a name for a
sandwich composed of Wonder bread and bologna. We can take
any experience and make it matter: put it in a barn or on a train,
make it back-lit or blast it with headlights. I make you a river,
so my love has somewhere to go.

I take the word *sacred* into me, and assign it to your mouth,
which is echoing my inner ear as the conch holds the ocean.
We are blind as a field. I am a maple tree wide as century, your kiss
the sun pouring through my green. Time rings me in radiance.
There is only this moment of enough. Stable as seed, your hands
hold all futures. My pollens drift to dust.

The little note cards on my knee are preserved petals. Levine claims
he hasn't met a poet who rivals Dickinson. We silence our beauty
inside the heavy book of Past. These cascading evasions we call
time and truth, around which we organize our disappearances,
return me to the cross-hatched convergence of afternoon and future.
The earth's thirst for metaphor rains you over my listening skin.
I breathe you in, then cry you out again. I write you down so
when the river returns, it will know to flow right through me.

As the Mountain Stands

you hold me in your mirror eyes
lake of great distances

until I see light as it asks to be seen
with reverence for the omissions

the wing hinges me to happiness
it is not yours or mine, but belongs

to flight. I would like to be
as long as shadow, the distance

of my own departure always in reach
I would like to welcome what won't arrive

as the mountain stands
you lie beside me, aligned

with the listening of my breath
which includes you to my ribs

from spine to chamber, you shine
a guidance that is mine

as writing weights the hand
but the word is free, we taste

all that was sacrificed
to the clean break

we can hear it in the singing
we can see it in the sheen of things

The Shadow of the Subjunctive

Dan says definition is death. Tonight I say: *enhungered.*
And still, I survive. This is the gift of language. It is the pyre,
and it is the phoenix.

Who was I before I arrived here on this page?

Last night I dreamed an editor responsible for midwifing my
essay did a cut and paste splicing of my story with Bill's – much
like Bill recently did deliberately with his own essay, weaving his
narrative through the italicized braid of his daughter's interpretation
of the same events. Except in my dream it was a little different.
This innocent ignition of story upon story resulted in an articulate
conception. I ended up pregnant from a cut and paste.

At the reading tonight, there was a man. I chose him for his back
turned away from me, and his beard. His shirt was wrong, but he
was young. He had time. I would like to say that I did something
brave or dangerous. But what I did was sit next to the drunken woman
who was sharing my pen. We kept it on the armrest between us, and
took turns scribbling notes on our respective papered knees. I wrote,
*Tomorrow when I go down to the river, I will be beautiful wherever
you kissed me,* from the poem read in both Spanish and English.

All translation is wrong, said Ursula LeGuin. *We have to get around
the shadow of the subjunctive.* What I want to know is: must we really?
Why can't we live there, in the half-light of "If I were" that keeps the
seashell between the speaker's hand and the return of ocean?
Tonight I am time's sand turned against its own downward ticking.
The hourglass is no measure of any certainty beyond containment.
I am the disappearance before it was counted.

There are horses being broken for insurance money. There are
pastures too sad to bear our weight. Where to go with this word
– *enhungered* – that has been pasted from one story into the next?

Leaving Buckhorn Springs

The farmland was an orchestra,
its ochres holding a baritone below
the soft bells of farmhouses,
altos of shadowed hills,
violins grieving the late
afternoon light. When I saw
the horses, glazed over with rain,
the battered old motorcycle parked
beside them, I pulled my car over
and silenced it on the gravel.
The rain and I were diamonds
displacing appetite with mystery.
As the horses turned toward me,
the centuries poured through
their powerful necks and my body
was the drum receiving the pulse
of history. The skin between me
and the world became the rhythm
of the rain keeping time with the sky
and into the music walked
the smallest of the horses. We stood
for many measures considering
each other, his eyes the quarter notes
of my heart's staccato. This symphony
of privacy and silence: this wildness
that the fence between us could not divide.

The Upstream Dream of the Salmon

I savor your extinguished life
slick with spawn and stream,

flesh of my appetite.
Dense with your destiny

unfolding inside of me, my leap
rises to meet the tide:

this thick, wet hope of my life.
The moon speaks through you.

Your night, my night.
Your sky, my sky. We answer

like twin dancers – sudden and strong.
We dream ourselves upstream.

This prayer is for all we are leaving behind:
the bear and his hot, heavy silences,

the waters that fight and carry us. This prayer
is for the forest that was not saved.

This prayer is for the mistakes that have
yet to be forgiven. This prayer is for the mosses

that soften the precipice of life's brevity
with dense beds of rest and reciprocity.

This prayer is for the faith
that we know how to begin again.

Nagoone Berries

The thorn bush holds her secrets
low to the ground.
In the privacy of rain
we kneel together,
heads bent to the berries.
Lush with leaf and hush
our voices settle like fog
among the unspoken
as we stain and bruise ourselves
with fruit. The earth drinks
and drinks until it spills open
and raw like a prayer book saturated
with God's desire for humanity.
We are a rhythm of choosing, crawling
along the bloated field through
necklaces of vine. The berries fall
wide-eyed into our collecting cup.
You carry that tender burden
of severed fruit home.
You stand over the stove,
cooking sacrifice
down to sugar.

Homeless. Hungry. God Bless.

It is spring, and there's too much of everything. Pollen drifts like unclaimed dreams over the throb of Friday afternoon traffic. The homeless man folded on the curb, holding his flimsy cardboard slogan, is the blossom burst through the split-skin bud of my heart. The parched earth has already starved our roots blind as I drive by in my large, empty car through the signals and sirens and light.

My cats devote their precision to death, feather my house with chase. Her fear stutters through my dreams; I find her days later in the sun room, a bouquet of feather and silence. I sit with her stilled terror. I sit with my own capture. Her death is my surrender. The homeless man's hunger chews through the night to the other side of my turning away.

There was a time I felt I could not survive the cruelties of this world until I understood that I am the cruelty. I am the house where the bird dies. I am the starvation that lives inside the cardboard collapse of faith. I breathe because breath has been given to me. In this agreement of city where lines divide yours and mine the bird and I lose our wings to the lineage of teachers unhinged from our cage of ribs. Together, we fill this house with praise. Death is its own painting. There is no stopping the sky.

In the absence of story, there is survival. In the absence of song, there is pavement. In the absence of truth, there is erosion. The tide becomes a thief.

If I could give to you these teeth of chewing, these bones of going forward. But I am homeless. I am hungry. God bless.

Plant Many. Grow Old.

Aisle of hurricane papered
in flowers. The militia of religion

has shred all gowns.
The heart beats now.

Shaken out, the Seven Plagues
hover like birds listening

to the soil turn with worm
travel. Under the crucible of fire,

inspiration shows its bones.
We are refined to shine.

Some seeds don't open.
Plant many. Grow old.

Thin your bounty
down to what you know.

A single thesis reaches
its leaves up into the overgrown.

She disappeared through the stiff pleats
of repeated ribs swelling into swans.

If the future could be contained
in lace, her mother would save

each seed in its zippered husk
instead of sending the guests home.

5-Element Acupuncture

A listening into David Ford

Repetition, metaphor, exaggeration. There's no time
to stop the car. The liver meridian abandons us to our
burning. The anger is our forest. An event wobbles the
map—uncharts us from destination. Take the message in
and chew each future equally into appearance. She braids
her head into order. The brick hits us where we are weak.
If we think in water, we are frozen with fear. The tears
come through the story you make of change. Here I am.
In the metal of abandonment, I find myself reflected.
Cold holding of disappearance. The fishing line sinks
into the solitude of seven. From the foundation, you build
a palace. We grow up alongside our siblings in different
families. Poisoned, my father stirred with his hands before
knowing that humor could be strangled to rage.
The bloody government. Map of intestine and float.
Because my mother breathed in my song when I breathed
out, the notes floated beyond certainty into darkness.
Color, sound, emotion, odor. Original wound emergent
in themes. Mountains of snow cupped into the deepest
emptinesses. Are you willing to heal? Beyond formula,
the kidney cries out for visibility. Let yourself be seen.

Divine Proportion

all life divides to 0.618
I feed you the sum

of my breasts each
floret aggregates past

ribs the formula
of your seeking we

spiral toward proportion
splicing time into the infinite

stability of increments
your breath my measurement

as seed dreams forest
you could build a world

on these breasts
whose effort should

not show the imposing
form of the absolute

Barn

Throw your shoulder
into the weight
of door lay down
your human
condition roll in
the sweet hay
of horse secrets
feast
on the nothing
you know

Eihwaz

"Once the decision is clear, the doing becomes effortless."
– The Book of Runes

The yew tree of yesterdays
narrows path to arrow.

Enter through obstacle
the new life unfolding.

I shed selves like petals.
Slowly, the weapon penetrates

history. As the brother starves
his family's famine, each lie runs

like water back to the source.
The telling of the story

is the building of the nest.
I set my house in order.

Feed the dogs.
Say my name.

It falls like the feather
of something hunted.

Spring Snow

something I have forgotten
or never known lives

in the deep well of you
I stretch like stem

into the emptiness
as petals flutter

to confetti in exchange
for the certainty of leaves

everything circles
back to where it started

my tongue turns
through you as the song

papers us in poetry
I follow your kiss

like time: through
the music into

the disappearance
of yours and mine

our first snow
of the season

Paiate Stone

let this moment be enough
ownership cannot survive

its illusions
beyond the fence

dividing wrong from right
shines the simple stone

of gratitude
the ripening of earth

the mind grown
quiet with time